WEDGES

Tatiana Tomljanovic

www.av2books.com

AV² provides enriched content that supplements and complements this book. Weigl's AV² books strive to create inspired learning and engage young minds in a total learning experience.

Your AV² Media Enhanced books come alive with...

Audio
Listen to sections of the book read aloud.

Key Words
Study vocabulary, and complete a matching word activity.

Video
Watch informative video clips.

Quizzes
Test your knowledge.

Go to **www.av2books.com**, and enter this book's unique code.

Embedded Weblinks
Gain additional information for research.

Slide Show
View images and captions, and prepare a presentation.

BOOK CODE

X235475

Try This!
Complete activities and hands-on experiments.

... and much, much more!

AV² by Weigl brings you media enhanced books that support active learning.

Published by AV² by Weigl
350 5th Avenue, 59th Floor
New York, NY 10118

Website: www.av2books.com   www.weigl.com

Library of Congress Cataloging in Publication Data

Tomljanovic, Tatiana
Wedges / Tatiana Tomljanovic
  p. cm.   (Simple machines)
  Summary: "Presents information on simple machines with a focus on wedges. Explains what a wedge is, how wedges work, and includes examples of past and present uses. Intended for third to fifth grade students.   Provided by publisher.
  Includes index.
  ISBN 978 1 62127 428 5 (hardcover alk paper)   ISBN 978 1 62127 434 6 (softcover alk paper)
  1. Wedges   Juvenile literature   I. Title
TJ1201.W44T65 2013
621.8'11 dc23
                  2012041026

Printed in the United States of America in North Mankato, Minnesota
1 2 3 4 5 6 7 8 9 0 17 16 15 14 13

042013
WEP040413

Project Coordinator Alexis Roumanis
Design: Mandy Christiansen

Photo Credits
Weigl acknowledges Getty Images as the primary photo supplier for this title. Page 22 A. R. Roumanis.

CONTENTS

All over the world, people use wedges to help them cut down trees. Saws, axes, and other cutting tools used by people in the logging industry all rely on the wedge in order to cut through wood.

What is a Wedge?

A wedge is a triangle-shaped device that is most often used to separate two objects. Wedges are also used to lift objects or to hold objects in place. Some wedges are narrow and sharp, while others are wide and rounded. However, all wedges work in a similar way.

The wedge is a simple machine. There are six simple machines, including the inclined plane, the lever, the pulley, the screw, and the wheel and axle. All simple machines make work easier. They do not have batteries or motors. They do not add any energy of their own to help people do work. Instead, simple machines work by changing the **effort** needed to perform a task.

■ Staples are a type of wedge that can cut through materials, such as fabrics or paper. They are used to hold things together.

Understanding Force

Force is a push or a pull that causes an object to move or change its direction. When an object is not moving, or at rest, all of the forces pushing or pulling it are balanced. This balance is called **equilibrium**.

When scientists study forces and how objects move, there are three measurements they need to know. They must know the object's **weight**, how fast it is moving, and the amount of force that is causing the object to move. Understanding forces, how forces affect objects, and how objects affect each other can make it easier to move objects.

Exercise is about overcoming force. A person's muscles provide the effort needed to run, walk, and jump.

What is Gravity?

Gravity is a force that pulls one object toward another. All objects have some gravity, though it is often very weak. An object's gravity is related to its mass. The more mass an object has, the greater its force of gravity and the pull it creates. Earth is a massive object, which means it has a strong gravity. This gravity pulls other objects toward the center of Earth.

Earth's gravity gives weight to an object's mass. A large rock has a great deal of mass. Earth's gravity pulls on this mass to create a heavy weight. A heavy weight needs a great force to make it move. This is why moving large objects often takes a great deal of effort.

MASS VS. WEIGHT

People often think mass and weight are the same, but they are very different. Mass is how much material an object contains. Weight is how strongly gravity pulls on an object. Mass is usually measured in kilograms, while weight is often measured in pounds.

A person with a mass of 91 kilograms weighs 200 pounds, but this is only true on Earth. This is because Earth's gravity pulls on a 91-kg mass with a force of 200 pounds. The Moon's much weaker gravity would only pull on a 91-kg mass with a force of 33 pounds. Also, if the person were to leave Earth on a space shuttle, he or she would become weightless. Even though the person would then weigh 0 pounds, his or her mass of 91 kg would not change.

Force Over Distance

In science, **work** happens when a force is used to move an object over a distance. For work to happen, the force must be applied in the same direction the object is moving.

In other words, lifting a rock off the ground is work because the force applied to pull the rock up is going in the same upward direction that the rock is moving. On the other hand, holding a rock while walking is not work. This is because the forward movement of walking is not related to the upward force that is holding the rock up.

■ Early farmers used a type of wedge called a plow to loosen soil in their fields. Farm animals provided the work needed to pull the plow through the soil. This allowed people to have larger farms and grow more crops than they could without a plow.

As the force needed to move an object increases, the work involved in moving it also increases. This also applies to distance. The amount of work needed to move the object increases as the distance the object must move increases.

Simple machines make doing work easier. They do this by changing the amount and the direction of the force needed to move the object. Though less force is needed, simple machines require moving a greater distance.

CALCULATING WORK

The amount of work needed to lift a 10-pound (4.5-kg) ball changes based on the distance it is lifted. To calculate the work, the weight of the ball is multiplied by the height it will be moved.

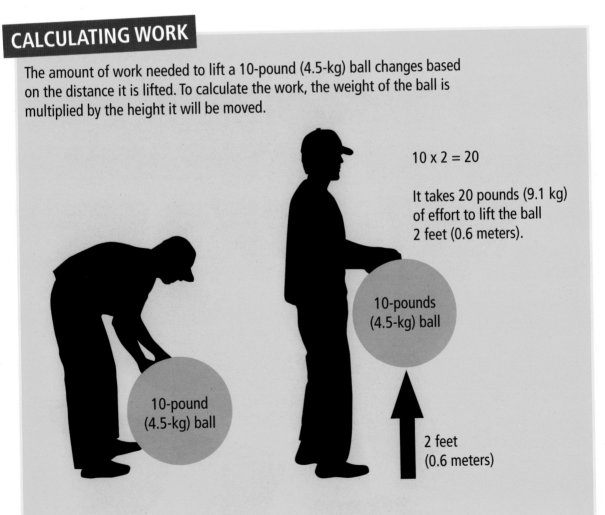

$10 \times 2 = 20$

It takes 20 pounds (9.1 kg) of effort to lift the ball 2 feet (0.6 meters).

10-pounds (4.5-kg) ball

10-pound (4.5-kg) ball

2 feet (0.6 meters)

How Wedges Work

Wedges offer a **mechanical advantage** that makes work easier. The mechanical advantage means that it will take less force to separate an object using a wedge than it would without using a wedge.

A force applied to the wide end of the wedge pushes the thin end through an object. This means that a wedge must move in order to do work. Simple wedges, such as axes and shovels, can be moved by hand.

When chopping wood, the downward force of the axe cuts into the wood. As the axe sinks into the wood, the thick part of the wedge starts to split the wood apart.

The mechanical advantage of a wedge comes from its shape. A force applied to the wide end is **concentrated** on the thin end as the wedge moves forward. This magnifies the force. As the wedge is pushed into the object, the wider parts of the wedge follow behind the thin edge. This pushes the sides of the object farther apart and splits it into two parts.

The shape of the wedge affects how it **efficient** it is. A long, thin wedge, such as a knife, will split an object with less force than a short, thick wedge, such as an axe. To split the object, however, the thin wedge must travel farther than the wide wedge. As with all simple machines, there is a trade-off between distance and force.

CALCULATING EFFORT

The amount of effort needed to split a block of wood apart changes based on the thickness of the wedge. What happens if the same force of 10 pounds (4.5 kg) is applied to three different wedges?

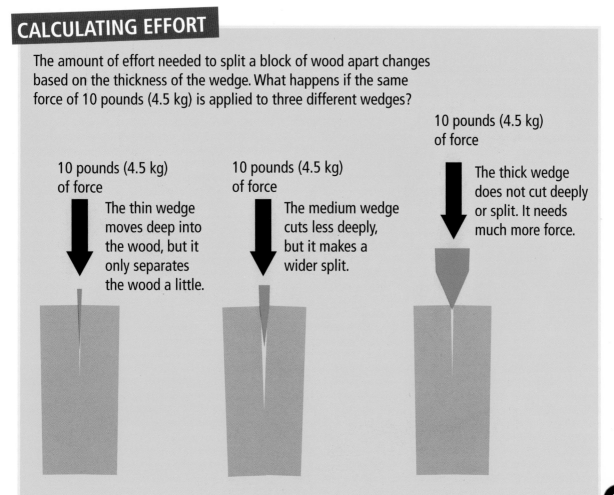

10 pounds (4.5 kg) of force

The thin wedge moves deep into the wood, but it only separates the wood a little.

10 pounds (4.5 kg) of force

The medium wedge cuts less deeply, but it makes a wider split.

10 pounds (4.5 kg) of force

The thick wedge does not cut deeply or split. It needs much more force.

Overcoming Friction

Friction is a force that is created when two surfaces come in contact with each other. A large amount of friction makes a strong grip between two surfaces. This can make it difficult to slide one object over the surface of another. Wedges may also be used to hold objects in place. A doorstop is a wedge that uses friction to hold a door open.

Wedges are often used to cut objects. The edge of a wedge will wear down over time. This is because of the friction created when a wedge cuts through an object. A knife that cuts soft objects, such as tomatoes, will stay sharper than an axe that splits hard objects, such as wood.

Knives are much thinner than most other kinds of wedges. This allows a knife to cut soft foods without squashing them.

Chisels are wedges that are used to chip away material, such as stone. A person strikes the wide end of the chisel with a hammer. This pushes the thin wedge shape against the stone, breaking off a small part of the stone. Chisels have been used for thousands of years. Stone masons used chisels to shape stones for building walls. Ancient artists used chisels to make sculptures. In the early 5th century BC, Greek sculptors began to use their chisels to make figures that were much more natural and realistic than any sculptures that had been made before this time.

Greek sculpture has inspired artists around the world. Today, many sculptors still use the hammer and chisel. With these tools, they can carve stone and other materials into works of art.

Using Wedges

Over the years, people have found many different ways to use wedges in daily life. In ancient Egypt, bronze wedges were used to break off blocks of rock for use in building. American Indians used a volcanic rock called **obsidian** to make both axes and **arrowheads**.

Wedges are used every day. Nails are wedges. They hold the walls of a house together. People sometimes use paper as a wedge to even a wobbly chair. A wedge on its side is a ramp. In this way, a wedge can be used to lift objects to different heights.

■ The wedge of a snowplow blade keeps roads clear of snow in winter.

Wedges in Action

People around the world use a variety of wedges every day.

JACKHAMMER

A jackhammer is used to break up hard surfaces, such as roads and sidewalks. It has a narrow, wedge-shaped blade. The motor in the jackhammer makes the blade hit the concrete over and over to break it apart.

ZIPPER

A zipper uses a wedge to pull together or separate two rows of teeth.

SCISSORS

The blades of the scissors are two wedges. When the scissors close, the blades cut the object between them.

TEETH

Shark teeth are razor sharp wedges. Sharks use their teeth to tear through food.

Wedges Timeline

2.6 million BC	8000 BC	6000 BC	4000 BC	2000 BC	100 AD	500	1600	1700	1800	1900	2000

1 **2** **3** **4** **5** **6** **7** **8** **9** **10**

1 **2.6 million BC**
The earliest human ancestors make wedges out of stones.

2 **8000 BC**
American Indians use stone wedges for cutting and hunting.

3 **3200 BC**
The Bronze Age begins in Europe. The first metal blades are produced.

4 **2000 BC**
The Mesopotamians invent a simple type of scissor that uses spring action.

5 **100 AD**
The Romans invent the modern scissor.

6 **500**
Farmers attach wheels to plows, improving farming.

7 **1634**
Galileo Galilei shows that simple machines do not create **energy**.

8 **1837**
John Deere produces the self-polishing plow.

9 **1917**
Gideon Sundback invents the modern-day zipper.

10 **1929**
Jacob Schick **patents** the first electric razor.

What is a Sculptor?

A sculptor is an artist who often works with clay, stone, or bronze. Using these materials, sculptors create **three-dimensional** objects, such as statues. Sculptors often go to an art school. Sometimes, they will work with an experienced artist to learn more about their art. Sculptors must learn how to use chisels and blades to create their art. It takes much skill and patience to be a sculptor. The smallest mistake can ruin a sculpture. Most sculptors work for themselves. They sell their art to the public. A company, government, or even an individual may hire a sculptor to create a special piece of art.

Gertrude Whitney

Gertrude Vanderbilt Whitney was an American sculptor. She was born in 1875 in New York. Whitney was very talented and was hired to create many special sculptures in the United States and around the world. She was a strong supporter of women in the arts. In 1929, Gertrude founded the Whitney Museum of American Art in New York. Today, it is one of the most well-known and respected art museums in the world.

■ Michelangelo completed his sculpture of David in 1504. The 17-foot (5.17-meter) statue was cut from one solid piece of marble. It took Michelangelo four years to finish.

The Two Basic Machines

The inclined plane and the lever are the most basic of all simple machines. In fact, all six simple machines can be seen as one of these two most basic machines.

TYPES OF INCLINED PLANE

The inclined plane is the simplest of the simple machines. Any slope, such as a hill, is an inclined plane.

A wedge is two inclined planes put together.

A screw is an inclined plane wrapped around a center bar.

TYPES OF LEVERS

A lever is a bar that rests on a pivot, or **fulcrum**. Pushing down on one end of the bar helps to lift a load on the other end of the bar.

A wheel and axle is a lever in which the bar circles around the fulcrum, or axle.

A pulley is a lever that uses a wheel for a fulcrum and a rope instead of a bar.

Complex Machines

Simple machines can be combined to make other kinds of machines. When two simple machines are combined, this new machine is often called a compound or complex machine. Wedges can be used together with other simple machines to create useful devices.

HELICOPTER

Helicopters have a series of thin wings. These wings are wedges that cut through the air when they spin, lifting the helicopter off the ground. The blades spin on an axle that is powered by a powerful engine.

CHAINSAW

The teeth of a chainsaw are sharp wedges. A motor spins a wheel on an axle, driving the chainsaw's teeth around.

CONSTRUCTION SHOVELS

Construction shovels are complex machines. The arm of the shovel is a lever, while the blade is a wedge. The wheel and axle help move the vehicle, while screws hold many parts together.

Seven Facts About Wedges

Pitch forks are a type of wedge used by farmers to lift hay.

Wedges used to hold tires in place are called chocks.

A sharp wedge is used in pencil sharpeners.

Wedges are used to cut and shape the planks of wood that make up a house.

In order for most cutting wedges to be useful, their edges must be kept sharp.

Some Aboriginal peoples use chisels to carve patterns of animals and people into long logs called totem poles.

The spoiler on a race car is a wedge. Its special shape helps keep the race car's tires on the ground at high speeds.

Wedges Brain Teasers

1   What is a wedge?

2   How many simple machines are there?

3   What sort of wedge does a sculptor or a stonemason use?

4   Who was Gideon Sundback?

5   Name at least three tools that are wedges.

6   What is a plow?

7   In science, what is the definition of work?

8   What part of the shark's body works like a wedge?

9   What kind of wedge is best for splitting wood?

10   What is it called when all forces acting on an object are balanced?

ANSWERS: 1. A wedge is a triangle-shaped tool with a sharp edge that can be used to separate two objects, lift an object, or hold an object in place **2.** There are six simple machines **3.** Chisels are used to shape stones **4.** Gideon Sundback was the inventor who created the zipper **5.** Knives, scissors, zippers, electric razors, doorstops, and teeth **6.** A plow is a kind of wedge that is dragged through soil to loosen it **7.** Work is defined as the force it takes to move an object **8.** Teeth are made up of differently shaped wedges **9.** A medium wedge will cut into wood and split it better than a thin or thick wedge. **10.** Equilibrium

Working with Wedges

Wedges come in handy when trying to fix everyday problems, such as evening out a wobbly chair or table. Try fixing a wobbly chair or table to see a wedge in action.

Materials Needed

piece of paper

wobbly chair, table, or desk

Directions

1 Find a chair or desk that does not sit evenly on the floor.

2 Fold a piece of paper in half four or five times.

3 Try placing the piece of paper under each chair leg.

4 Did you put the folded edge or the loose edges of the paper under the wobbly leg of the chair? Did the paper wedge help to steady the chair?

Key Words

arrowheads: wedge-shaped pieces of rock or metal attached to the end of an arrow

concentrated: focused on a small area

efficient: getting a desired result from as little effort as possible

effort: the force being used to move a load

energy: power needed to do work

equilibrium: a state when all the forces acting on an object are balanced

friction: the result of one surface rubbing against another surface

fulcrum: the point where a lever turns

mechanical advantage: a measure of how much easier a task is made when a simple machine is used

obsidian: a black, glass-like rock formed by rapidly cooling lava

patents: receives a grant from the government to make, use, or sell something over a certain period of time

three-dimensional: having length, height, and depth

weight: the force of gravity's pull on an object's mass

work: force applied over distance to move an object

Index

Log on to www.av2books.com

AV² by Weigl brings you media enhanced books that support active learning. Go to www.av2books.com, and enter the special code found on page 2 of this book. You will gain access to enriched and enhanced content that supplements and complements this book. Content includes video, audio, weblinks, quizzes, a slide show, and activities.

AV² Online Navigation

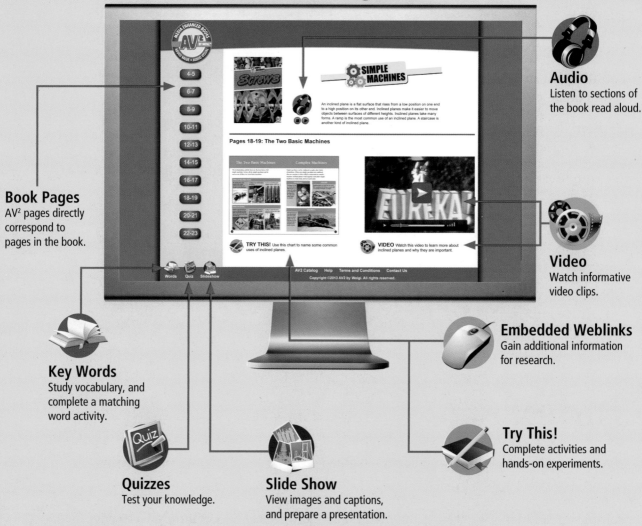

Book Pages
AV² pages directly correspond to pages in the book.

Audio
Listen to sections of the book read aloud.

Video
Watch informative video clips.

Key Words
Study vocabulary, and complete a matching word activity.

Embedded Weblinks
Gain additional information for research.

Quizzes
Test your knowledge.

Slide Show
View images and captions, and prepare a presentation.

Try This!
Complete activities and hands-on experiments.

AV² was built to bridge the gap between print and digital. We encourage you to tell us what you like and what you want to see in the future.

Sign up to be an AV² Ambassador at www.av2books.com/ambassador.

J
621.811
T

Tomljanovic, Tatiana
Wedges

cly
11/24/14